Curio: of East Sussex

A County Guide
to the Unusual

by

David Arscott

S.B. Publications

By the same author: *Explore Sussex*
Co-author (with Warden Swinfen): *Hidden Sussex*
People of Hidden Sussex
Hidden Sussex Day by Day
Hidden Sussex — the Towns

First published in 1991 by S.B. Publications
Unit 2, The Old Station Yard, Pipe Gate, Nr. Market Drayton
Shropshire TF9 4HY

British Library Cataloguing in Publication Data
Arscott, David
  Curiosities of East Sussex:
  A county guide to the unusual.
  I. Title
  91422504858

  ISBN 1-870708-87-3

Typeset and printed by Delmar Press (Colour Printers) Ltd., Nantwich, Cheshire
Bound by John Sherratts (Manchester) Ltd.

CONTENTS

Front cover: John Harmer gravestone terracotta at Cade Street.

Back cover: Mummified cats, Stag Inn, Hastings.

Title page: Ship's figurehead outside the Star Inn, Alfriston.

INTRODUCTION

Let us delight in inconsequential things, the merest offcuts of a county's history, the time-worn relics of those men and women who have helped to shape it. Let us be thankful for the tenacity of old brick walls, of gnarled and ancient trees, of memorials whose faded inscriptions tell stories still well worth the hearing. This book is an unashamed addition to the 'fancy that!' body of local literature to which I have been pleased to contribute from time to time over recent years. It does (perhaps on the sly) attempt to offer a kind of history lesson, but one such as none of us surely enjoyed at school — quirky, fragmentary, random.

To the curious all things are curious; to the dull, dull. All I can plead for what you find illustrated here is that some are strange in themselves; others are unique survivors; most have something to say about the time in which they were created and the people who made them. All of them may be seen without breaking the law of trespass, but a few do have to be viewed from a distance. In the case of some of the follies this is no bad thing, since their decay is all too sadly apparent at close quarters.

Sussex is rich in the unusual, and it has been necessary to pick and choose. Where space allows, I refer in the text to similar features elsewhere in the county and to other curiosities in the near vicinity, for I hope very much that you will feel inspired to investigate further. Once you learn that a humble standpipe hidden among trees is the sole reminder of a long-gone industry; that a remote tower was once part of a vanished mansion; that a strangely inappropriate statue used to stand outside St Paul's Cathedral; then you begin to notice oddities at every turn and to ask more questions than can possibly be answered.

This book comes, therefore, with a warning: sniffing out curiosities may well prove addictive. Open its pages only if you relish the prospect of a lifetime's treasure-hunting along the by-ways of historic Sussex.

David Arscott

In preparation: Curiosities of West Sussex.

RYE

A MURDERER'S SKULL

Access: In an upstairs room of the town hall. Ask at the town clerk's office below.
Map reference: TQ922203

On a dark and blustery night in 1742 a butcher named John Breeds decided to kill the mayor of Rye, Thomas Lamb, who had fined him for giving short weight. The man he actually stabbed in the churchyard was Lamb's brother-in-law, Allen Grebell, who had borrowed the intended victim's cloak. Breeds was hanged for the crime in 1743 and his body left to rot in a cage out on the marshes. We can only guess what happened to the rest of his bones (superstitious women used to collect them as cures for various pains and diseases), but the top of Breeds' skull remains to this day in the cage.

A grave slab set into the floor of the church records Grebell's fate, killed 'by the cruel stab of a sanguinary butcher'. The unlucky Grebell is said to haunt Lamb House, which later became the home of the novelist Henry James.

Note St. Mary's church turret clock, said to be the oldest in the country, and the quarter boys who ring the chimes on the quarter-hours. The clock is still worked by its original 350-year-old mechanism. The clock's face and quarter boys were added in 1760, and the 18ft-long pendulum swings down inside the church tower.

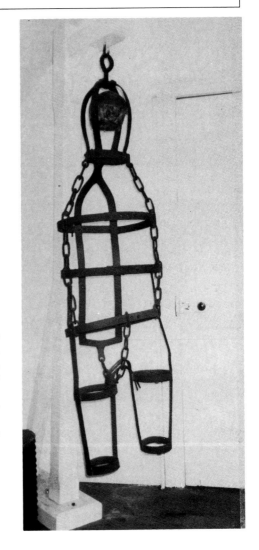

1

RYE

WATER CISTERN, ST MARY'S CHURCH

> *Access:* In the Churchyard.
> *Map reference:* TQ922203

St . Mary's church stands at the
highest point of a hilltop town
which must have suffered
considerable water problems in
days gone by. This explains the
otherwise bizarre situation of this
equally strange oval building. A
superb example of bricklaying
skills, it was built in 1735 to hold
water raised by a horse-powered
pump from the bottom of town.
Most of the cistern lies
underground, and there's a gauge
to show the amount of water
being stored. The townspeople
were supplied through a network
of pipes and channels.

*For an even earlier water source,
peek into the (private) garden of
the house called Queen's Well in
Deadmans Lane. Elizabeth 1
stopped to drink here in 1573, the
day after she left her shoes at
NORTHIAM. A plaque on the
wall behind the well is dated 1588.
(See also page 7).*

RYE HARBOUR

LIFEBOAT MEMORIAL

Access: Follow the Rye Harbour signs from Rye. The church is about a mile along the road on your right, and the memorial is at the far side of the churchyard.
Map reference: TQ938203

This memorial commemorates one of the worst lifeboat disasters of all time. At 4.50 on the morning of 15 November, 1928, the *Mary Stanford* was launched from Rye Harbour in a terrible storm to go to the rescue of a Latvian steamer. Within minutes signals were fired to recall her since news had come that the ship's crew had been taken aboard another vessel. The lifeboat crew failed to see the signals because of the conditions at sea, and all seventeen men aboard were drowned when the boat overturned. Rye Harbour was a tiny community: many of the men were related to one another, and there was scarcely a family in the port village not touched by death.

The inscription on the monument reads: 'We have done that which was our duty to do.'

RYE FOREIGN

CORDBAT COTTAGE

Access: Rye Foreign lies 3 miles north-west of Rye on the A268. The cottage is on your left, immediately opposite the Hare and Hounds public house. *Map reference:* TQ898225

In the Rev. William Parish's *Dictionary of the Sussex Dialect,* published in 1875, cordbats are defined as 'large pieces of wood, roots, etc., set up in stacks'. What better name, then, for this gloriously distinctive piece of vernacular architecture? The walls are, indeed, made of thin logs set on end and packed around with (one guesses) a mixture of earth and cowdung. The thatched roof is an unusual touch, too.

Parish was vicar of Selmeston, east of Lewes, and is buried in the churchyard there. His dictionary, augmented and republished in 1957, is humorous as well as scholarly. He notes, for instance, a brass inscription at Selmeston to Henry Rogers, 'a painefull preacher in this church' - noting that the word meant 'painstaking' in earlier days.

IDEN

KENT/SUSSEX BOUNDARY STONE

Access: The village of Iden itself lies just north of Rye, but for the boundary marker you need to follow the Military Road out of Rye. Take the north east fork north of the Landgate. The Royal Military Canal will appear on your right, and the stone is on the bank above you.
Map reference: TQ940243

That apparently insignificant channel of water you see in the picture is the Kent Ditch, the boundary between the two counties. The stone was erected in 1806 to commemorate the creation of the Royal Military Canal. It's inscribed with the date and the county names.

The canal, designed to thwart Napoleon's invasion plans, originally ran from Hythe in Kent to Rye, but was later extended westwards to Pett. (see page 10)

PLAYDEN

FLEMISH BREWER'S GRAVESLAB

> *Access:* In Playden church, a mile north of Rye on the A268
> *Map reference:* TQ920216

Who was Cornelis Roetmans? A black stone slab of about 1530 is our evidence, and fairly conclusive it is, too. The stone is thought to be of carboniferous limestone imported from the Liege area of Belgium, where similar inscriptions can be found: *Hier is begraven Cornelis Roetmans bidt voer de ziele* translates as 'Here is buried Cornelis Roetmans pray for his soul'. And the drawings (originally inlaid with brass) depicting two casks with a crossed mashstick and fork? Yes, Mr. Roetmans was a Flemish brewer.

Another question in the same vein; Who was Jhone Colins? In Burwash church there's a badly worn cast-iron slab with that name on it, seemingly in Lombardic script. This probably refers to a John rather than a Joan, and the supposition is that he may have been an ironmaster during the time the industry flourished here. Such men were prosperous, as you can tell by visiting Rudyard Kipling's former home, Batemans, in Burwash - thought to have been built by an iron-master in the seventeenth century.

NORTHIAM

QUEEN ELIZABETH'S OAK

> *Access:* Northiam is about 8 miles north-west of Rye. The oak is at the top of the village green, alongside the A28.
>
> *Map reference:* TQ830245

Good Queen Bess came to Sussex in 1573 to review the fleet at Rye, and she left a pair of shoes behind her after enjoying a picnic under this very tree at Northiam. A sign on the tree reminds us of the Sussex saying that 'our oaks are a thousand years living and a thousand years dying', and suggests that this specimen may be more than a thousand years old.

We're on more certain ground regarding the Queen's footwear; 'She changed her shoes of green damask silk with a heel 2½" high and a sharp toe, at this spot, and left them behind as a memento of her visit. They are still in existence and are shown on special occasions.'

For admirers of venerable trees, two ancient yews in East Sussex: at Wilmington and at Crowhurst, near Battle, with girths of 23ft. and more than 40 ft. respectively.

7

WINCHELSEA

WESLEY'S TREE

Access: About 2 miles south-west of Rye on the A259. The tree is just outside the west wall of the churchyard.
Map reference: TQ904174

It's not as old as Elizabeth's oak, but this ash at Winchelsea is the scion of one under which John Wesley preached his last open-air sermon on the same spot. The original was struck by lightning.

Wesley's journal for October 7, 1790, refers to it: 'I went over to that poor skeleton of ancient Winchelsea; it is beautifully situated on the top of a steep hill and was regularly built in broad streets, crossing each other, and encompassing a very large square; in the midst of which was a large church, now in ruins. I stood under a large tree, on the side of it, and called to most of the inhabitants of the town "The Kingdom of heaven is at hand; repent and believe the Gospel". It seemed as if all that heard were, for the present, almost persuaded to be Christians.'

You'll find another tree with a famous connection in Hastings Old Town – a mulberry grown from a cutting taken from Shakespeare's very own tree in Stratford-on-Avon. The actor David Garrick brought it here. Climb Tamarisk Steps by the Dolphin Inn, and there's a sign guiding you to a little garden.

WINCHELSEA

TOWN WELL

Access: In Castle Street, a minute's walk north-east from the church.
Map reference: TQ906175

This town well, built in 1831, was the only one within the walls of Winchelsea, which speaks for its importance. It was in use within living memory. One of the two large notice boards affixed to it gives the opening times: from 6 a.m until 7 p.m. daily, except for the Sabbath. The other, dated July 1872, suggests that the locals weren't always on their best behaviour: 'All persons are strictly cautioned against throwing anything whatsoever down the town well as the Police have order to report immediately any act of nuisance so that the offenders may be prosecuted.'

PETT

ROYAL MILITARY CANAL

> *Access:* Follow the A259 west from Rye and turn off left on the narrow coastal road to Winchelsea Beach. After a little more that two miles the road turns inland at Cliff End. The canal begins almost immediately on your right.
>
> *Map reference:* TQ889134

This attractively overgrown little waterway was built for military purposes. It's the start - or, more accurately, the end - of the Royal Military Canal. In 1804 Lt. Col John Brown had the bright idea of creating a broad moat as a defence barrier against invasion by the forces of Napoleon. Pitt's government rushed the scheme through at vast expense, starting in Kent and eventually finishing here. It was wider then than now, but it's hard to understand how an army which had successfully crossed the English Channel would have been balked by a canal less than thirty feet wide. You can follow parts of it on foot, but the way to see it all is by canoe.

Other defences built against the feared Napoleonic invasion include The Redoubt fortress at Eastbourne and a string of Martello towers along the coast - among them the one at SEAFORD. (see page 56).

HASTINGS

BELFRY RHYMES

Access: Just inside All Saints Church, at the top of All Saints Street.
Map reference: TQ828099

This curious 18-century warning in verse seems to have been aimed at bell ringers who arrived late, so still wearing 'spur or hat':

This is a belfry, that is free
for all those that civil be
and if you please to chime or ring
it is a very pleasant thing.

There is no musick played or sung
like unto Bells when theyr well rung
then ring your bells well if you can
Silence is best, for every man.

But if you ring in spur or hat
sixpence you pay be sure of that
and if a bell you overthrow
pray pay a groat before you go.

You snapped the wooden stop if you 'overthrew' a bell, which would appear to be shamingly unprofessional conduct. The fine, however, was less than that imposed on the hat and spur wearers!

The Doom painting over the chancel arch here is regarded as one of the finest medieval wallpaintings in the country.

HASTINGS

JOHN ARCHDÈADON'S GRAVESTONE

Access: To the left of the entrance of All Saints Church in the Old Town.
Map reference: TQ828099

This gravestone tells a terrible story. Nine-year-old John Archdeacon died on June 5, 1820:

Here lies an only darling boy
Who was his widow'd mother's joy,
Her grief and sad affliction prove
How tenderly she did him love.

In childish play he teased a mule
Which rag'd its owner's angry soul
And thro' whose cruel blows and spleen
This child so soon a corpse was seen.

This Mother now is left to mourn
The loss of her beloved Son
Tho' sighs and tears will prove in vain
She hopes in Heaven to meet again.

The mule's owner, William Picknell, was charged at Lewes Assizes with 'feloniously killing and slaying' the lad, but was acquitted.

HASTINGS

MUMMIFIED CATS

Access: In the Stag Inn, near the top of All Saints Street.
Map reference: TQ827098

A grisly sight greets customers of the Stag Inn - the blackened bodies of two cats discovered in one of the chimneys of this Elizabethan building during 19th-century restoration work. It may be that the poor animals became trapped there and that their carcasses were simply preserved by the smoke. Another possibility, however, is that they were sacrificed in propitiation of whatever evil force it may be that brings disaster to a home: other examples have reportedly been discovered in the Old Town.

HASTINGS

NET SHOPS

Access: On the Stade, at the eastern end of the sea-front
Map reference: TQ827094

The so-called net shops, first erected in Tudor times, were traditionally used by fishermen for the drying of their nets. Today's synthetic materials are easier to deal with, but these tall wooden structures, unique in Britain, survive as storage sheds for a remarkably resilient fishing fleet.

At the the foot of All Saints Street, look out for a giant winkle. Local fishermen formed the Winkle Club in 1899 to help the underprivileged, and any member found not to be carrying his winkle badge when challenged has to pay a fine to charity.

HASTINGS

LOGIE BAIRD MEMORIAL

Access: In Queen's Arcade, off Queen's Road opposite the Town Hall.
Map reference: TQ817095

It was on January 19, 1924, that television was born. On that day John Logie Baird successfully transmitted two 'pictures by wireless' - a Maltese cross and the hand of his assistant, Victor Mills. Baird's workshop has gone, but a plaque marks the place where the seminal event happened.

HASTINGS

PULPITT GATE

Access: Near the foot of All Saints Street.
Map reference: TQ826095

The imposing stone window set into the house called Pulpitt Gate is but one of its oddities. The building is a bizarre modern fabrication, featuring a Jacobean staircase, some stained glass windows, and a disused well in the dining room. The window came from Normanhurst Court, built at Catsfield, near Battle, by the famous railway contractor Thomas Brassey. Normanhurst, demolished in 1954, was itself something of a sport, being designed to look like a French chateau. It's possible, therefore, that the window actually came from France in the first place.

Another very strange building is The Piece of Cheese, a little way up All Saints Street on the right. It's named for its shape (the builder had only a narrow, triangular piece of land to work on) but the walls have been painted an appropriate yellow.

HASTINGS

CANNONBALL IN CHURCH TOWER

Access: St Clement's Church, off High Street in the Old Town.
Map reference: TQ824096

A case of 'spot the genuine cannon ball'. A Dutch warship is said to have fired on St Clement's church during the hostilities between the two countries during the 17th century. Rather than dislodge the shot from its resting place high in the tower, the church authorities decided that it would be simpler to install a matching one on the other side of the window. If you think the story unlikely you need to think of a good alternative reason for the unusual design feature.

HASTINGS

THE HASTINGS RARITIES

Access: In Hastings Museum, Cambridge Road. *Map reference:* TQ809095

That's a night heron in the centre of the picture – not a common sight in East Sussex. The other birds in this museum case would be a local ornithologist's dream, too. They're among the so-called Hastings Rarities, birds never seen in this part of the world until passed to the authorities by the taxidermist George Bristow. Some years after his death in 1939 the stuffed birds became the centre of a scandal. Experts declared the affair a hoax and some twenty species were struck off the List of British Birds. Bristow, for the record, always maintained his innocence.

An even more famous hoax is commemorated in the name of the Piltdown Man pub (formerly The Lamb) at Piltdown, seven miles north of Lewes. Charles Dawson, a respected solicitor and a member of several learned societies, was the man who unearthed the bones of the supposed 'missing link' between the apes and man. Many have claimed that he was innocent, too.

ST LEONARDS

JAMES BURTON'S PYRAMID

Access: In a small family graveyard off West Hill Road above St Leonards
Church
Map reference: TQ797089

The builder James Burton, responsible for developing prestigious areas of London such as Regent Street, Bloomsbury and St John's Wood, had a dream one night of a garden city by the sea. He was already in his late sixties, but in 1828 he nevertheless began the building of his maritime paradise, St Leonards, and his son Decimus later completed the task. The Burton graveyard is on a high point overlooking the sea and St Leonard's Church, and an impressive pyramid sits at the centre of it. Why the unusual shape? Family tradition has it that Burton's notion was to evade the eastern curse: 'May jackasses sit on your father's grave'.

19

ST LEONARDS

GALILEAN BOAT PULPIT

Access: St Leonards Church, just off the sea front
Map reference: TQ796088

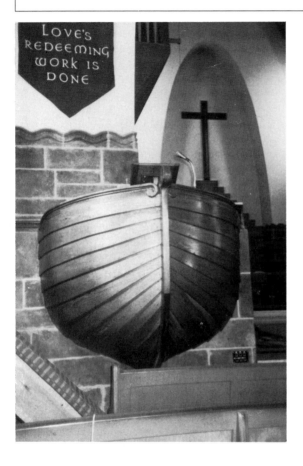

Another St Leonards dream produced this unique pulpit, in the form of a boat's prow which would have been familiar to Jesus of Nazareth. The night after the former church here was destroyed by a German V-1 in July 1944, the rector dreamed that he saw Christ preaching in a boat on the Lake of Galilee. What better design for the pulpit of the reborn church than just such a boat? It seems to have become a personal obsession in the face of some ridicule and considerable logistical difficulties, but twelve years later the pulpit was finished - fashioned by a Galilean craftsman from oak cut from the forest of Baashan.

BALDSLOW

STATUE OF QUEEN ANNE

Access: North of Hastings in the grounds of Holmhurst St Mary, now a convent, but visible from outside. Take the B2093 from Ore and the statue is on your left.
Map reference: TQ800130

Augustus Hare was a 19th-century author who specialised in books of foreign travel, but one of his strangest journeys must have been the one from London to his home at Baldslow with this vast statue of Queen Anne. Does it seem familiar? It stood outside St Paul's Cathedral until the weather took its toll and it was replaced by the replica which is there to this day. Hare came across the rejected statue in a stonemason's yard in Southwark and thought it would be just the thing to grace the grounds of Holmhurst. The figures at the Queen's feet represent Britannia, Ireland, France and America.

BATTLE

WHERE KING HAROLD FELL

Access: Battle Abbey
Map reference: TQ748157

The great 1066 confrontation between Saxons and Normans took place not at Hastings, as its common name would have you believe, but on unpopulated terrain some miles to the north-west. The Conqueror decided that an abbey should be built on the site in commemoration of his great victory, and that the altar of the abbey church should rise over the very spot at which Harold fell. When Henry VIII declared war on the wealthy religious institutions Battle Abbey was given to Sir Anthony Browne, who dismantled it. Stones from the ruins were used in local buildings (see the Bull Inn) and especially in Brown's new house – now a school in the grounds. The church was destroyed, but a stone marks the location of the high altar.

In the churchyard of St Mary the Virgin, a little to the east, is the tomb of a remarkable man. Isaac Ingall was butler at the Abbey for all of 95 years, and died in 1798 at the age of 120.

BEXHILL

THE BEXHILL STONE

> *Access:*   In St Peter's Church, mounted in a case on the south side of the tower.
> *Map reference:* TQ745081

The Bexhill Stone, discovered under the nave floor during restoration work in 1878, is something of a mystery. It's thought to be the lid of a reliquary, which was a container for the relics of a saint. Why it should have been discarded is one puzzle. Another is its place of origin: the stone itself is of a kind found only in the north of England, and the elaborate carving suggests a Celtic influence.

NINFIELD

VILLAGE STOCKS

Access: On a small triangle of grass near to the church on the A271 towards Boreham Street.
Map reference: TQ707124

Not only stocks, but a whipping post, too. Few of these survive in East Sussex, presumably because they were made of perishable wood. The Ninfield stocks are of cast- and wrought- iron, possibly made at Ashbournham in the days when a furnace and a forge flourished there, as in so many parts of the Sussex weald. There are four holes for ankles and four wrist clamps.

It was at this spot that a notable case of wife-selling occurred in 1790, when a man disposed of his soul-mate for half a pint of gin. In accordance with tradition, she arrived in the company of two witnesses with a halter about her neck. A contemporary report noted that 'she appeared mightily delighted about the ceremony, and the hopeful pair departed filled with joy and expectation from the happy union'.

Standard Hill, near Ninfield, is reputed to be the spot where William I erected his standard after the Battle of Hastings..

EASTBOURNE

EDWARDIAN URINALS

Access: In Hampden Park. One close to each of the park's two entrances.
Map reference: TQ602020

What the ladies did one hesitates to guess, but gentlemen were well catered for when Hampden Park was created as a showpiece in Edwardian Eastbourne. These MacParlane patent urinals are no longer in use, but it's still possible to admire the patterned cast-iron panels.

EASTBOURNE

LUSHINGTON MEMORIAL

Access: In St Mary's Church, Old Town.
Map reference: TV598995

To survive the terrible Black Hole of Calcutta and yet to be 'inhumanly murdered' only a few years later seems the most wretched luck, but such was the fate which befell young Henry Lushington. As his memorial tells, he sailed for Bengal at the age of sixteen in the service of the India Company:

In ye Year 1756, by a melancholy Revolution, He was with Others to ye Amount of 146 forced into a Dungeon at CALCUTTA so small that 23 only escaped Suffocation. He was one of ye Survivors, but reserved for greater Misery, for by a Subsequent Revolution in the Year 1763 He was with 200 more taken Prisoners at PATNA, and after a tedious Confinement being singled out with JOHN ELLIS and WILLIAM HAY Esq. was by the Order of the Nabob COSSIM ALLY KAWN and under ye Direction of One SOMEROO, an Apostate European, deliberately and inhumanly murdered: But while ye Seapoys were performing their savage Office on ye first mentioned Gentleman, fired with a generous Indignation at the Distress of his Friend, he rushed upon his Assassins unarmed, & seizing One of their Scimitars killed Three of Them and wounded Two Others, until at length oppressed with Numbers he greatly fell.

Lushington was only twenty six. One of those killed with him, William Hay, came from the East Sussex village of Glynde.

EASTBOURNE

VICTORIAN LICENCE PLATES

Access: At the foot of the wall below the Wish Tower in King Edward's Parade.
Map reference: TV614983

Once you know that the little iron discs to be found at pavement level in various parts of Eastbourne were Victorian licence plates, you can have a little amusement guessing what the letters referred to. This one, *GCS,* indicates that here was once a goat chaise stand.

The principal places to look are near the Wish Tower, outside Eastbourne College in Grange Road, and along the wall of St Saviour's Church in South Street. You'll find *HCS, BCS, MCS, SPS, SDS* and *LPS* - and in case you'd like to work them out for yourself, I shall make everything plain within a relevant entry in the forthcoming *Curiosities of West Sussex.*

Situated on the wall of the promenade facing the handstand is a memorial plaque to John Wesley Woodward; one of the heroic musicians who went down in the 'Titanic' in April 1912. He played the cello in the Grand Hotel orchestra, the Duke of Devonshire's orchestra and the Eastbourne municipal orchestra.

PEVENSEY

A PRISONER'S GRAFFITO

Access: In the Court House museum in the High Street, Pevensey, east of Eastbourne.

Map reference: TQ647049

Whatever Thomas Hall was locked up for, it surely can't have been drunkenness. The simple message he carved on his cell door (THOMAS HALL WAS PUT IN JAIL DEC-EMBER 22 1823) shows control as well as artistic flair. One of the two cells below what was 'once the smallest town hall in England' may still be inspected, but its door is more recent; the remaining part of the earlier one decorated by Mr. Hall is now on show in the museum above.

The museum also contains the oldest existing Cinque Ports Seal.

For a similar graffito, visit Horsham museum in West Sussex, A floorboard from the former country gaol is inscribed with a prisoner's initials.

EAST DEAN

BELLE TOUT LIGHTHOUSE

> *Access:* Take the Beachy Head road from East Dean, some 3 miles west of Eastbourne. After Birling Gap there's a lay-by on your right and a footpath up to the lighthouse.
> *Map reference:* TV563955

The first shore light for sailors along this part of the coast was provided early in the 18th century by Jonathan Darby, the vicar of East Dean, who had a tunnel excavated through the chalk cliffs and regularly lit a beacon in a cave looking out to sea. More than a century passed before the building of a permanent lighthouse, Belle Tout, in 1828. The granite for its construction was dragged across the Downs by teams of oxen. Alas, it proved to be a failure: although the beam from the 47ft.-high circular stone tower could be seen 23 miles out to sea, it was obscured by low cloud and mist for about six months every year. A new lighthouse was built at the foot of Beachy Head in 1902, and Belle Tout became what estate agents would no doubt call a private residence of character.

POLEGATE

TOWER MILL

Access: In Park Croft, just west of the A22 south of Polegate crossroads.
Map reference: TQ581041

A windmill in the middle of a housing estate is something of an oddity, but there's no doubt which came first: this brick tower mill, now completely restored.

The mill was built for Joseph Seymour, a farmer, in 1817. Its last miller, Albert Ovenden, died in 1973 at the age of 71, and for his funeral the sweeps (as the sails are known in Sussex) were set in the St George's cross position - a miller's traditional distress signal.

Next to the mill is a small museum containing many items connected with its operation and maintenance.

WILLINGDON

VILLAGE PUMP

Access: Near the top of Wish Hill, off the A22 on the western outskirts of Eastbourne.

Map reference: TQ589020

Look closely at the patterned walls of this pump house and you'll see that dozens of cows' knuckle bones have been used to form two panels within the flints. We know that the village slaughterhouse provided the bones when the building was erected in 1880, but why the design was chosen is a mystery. It seems that before weathering took its toll there were once even more of them. The pump is on the site of a traditional 'dipping hole', where a natural spring emerges at the foot of the Downs.

FRISTON

TAPSELL GATE

Access: At the entrance to the churchyard.
Map reference: TV552982

The Mountfield carpenter John Tapsell gave his name to a distinctive type of gate which pivots on a central pillar, thus rendering hinges and fastenings unnecessary. It is assumed that they were designed to prevent animals from straying into the churchyards, and they were easier to carry a coffin through. Tapsell gates are something of a rarity but you can find three fairly close together at Friston, East Dean and Jevington churches. Jevington is a particularly puzzling example as it has a step in the centre so it can be used as a stile, but as the gate opens easily and there is no fastening, its purpose seems obscure.

Friston pond, just beyond the church, has a peculiar claim to fame - reputedly the first village pond to be listed as an ancient monument.

JEVINGTON

A STRANGE PLAQUE.

> *Access:* In the church
> *Map reference:* TQ561015

In which year did Nathaniel Collier die? His black marble memorial in Jevington church gives the alternatives of 1691 and 1692. This reflects, not uncertainty about exactly when he went to meet his Maker, but the long-raging controversy about the calendar itself. Under the Old Style, then still in use in England, the year began on March 25; whereas the New style introduced by Pope Gregory XIII in 1582, and adopted by the Roman Catholic countries of Europe, counted from January 1. The former rector was a non-juror, one of those beneficed clergy who refused to take the oath of allegiance to the Protestant William and Mary in 1689. Perhaps, with his powerful religious convictions, he liked to believe that he took to his death-bed in the year 1692, whatever the secular authorities might decree.

By a remarkable coincidence, the Worcestershire volume of this series records an identical example in the church at Rous Lench. The stone mason would appear to be the same man, and the date is, again, 169½.

ALFRISTON

MARKET CROSS

Access: In the centre of the village.
Map reference: TQ521032

It's little more than a stump today, but this is the only surviving market cross in the whole of East Sussex. It was demolished by a lorry several years ago, but the restored edifice stands proudly enough at the centre of this much-visited village.

Among the buildings to look out for in Alfriston are the 14th-century Clergy House, the first property ever bought by the National Trust (for £10 in 1896), and the Smugglers Inn, once owned by Stanton Collins, a butcher known to be a smuggler but actually deported for sheep-stealing. This isn't the village's oldest inn, but it's remarkable for having six stair-cases and such a plethora of exits and entrances that one small room has no fewer than five doors.

34

ALFRISTON

VILLAGE LOCK-UP

Access: In the car park close to the Heritage Centre.
Map reference: TQ519033

No records survive to estasblish what function this little building once served. A map of 1874 marks it as a dovecote, but it's sufficiently similar to examples in other parts of the country to suggest that this was, in fact, Alfriston's lock-up, where the local hotheads were left to cool down before the administration of justice. Not a comfortable place to spend the night.

WILMINGTON

THE LONG MAN

> Access: Best seen from the car park of Wilmington Priory, off the A27, eight miles north-west of Eastbourne. The South Downs Way runs just above the Long Man, and there's a convenient lay-by up the hill from the priory on your right.
> *Map reference:* TQ543035

He's said to be the largest representation of the human form anywhere in the world, all of 230 feet tall, but nothing of any consequence is known about the Long Man of Wilmington. Perhaps he was created in the Bronze Age or connected with the war god Odin, as some have claimed, but he may be of much more recent origin. He's now outlined in white blocks.

Take the footpath which runs above the Long Man's head and you come across a pock-marked area of downland. This is one of the sites at which neolithic men sank mines 40 feet deep in the chalk for the extraction of flints.

Sussex has another chalk figure, and not very far away. Take the minor road between Litlington and West Dean and you'll see a white horse cut into the south-east slope of the hill called High and Over. The 90 ft.- long figure is said to have been cut by three local men in 1924 during ten hours of moonlight night. It was camouflaged during the second world war and renovated in 1949.

LULLINGTON

THE SMALLEST CHURCH IN SUSSEX

Access: By a footpath off the minor road from Wilmington to Litlington.
Map reference: TQ528031

The 'smallest church' tag is perhaps a bit of a cheat, since this is only the chancel of a decayed medieval building, the foundations of which lie half-buried in the turf to the west. The surviving portion of the church is fifteen feet square, seats eighteen people and is still used for regular worship. It contains a font, lectern and altar housed within flint walls broken by lancet windows and topped by a tiled roof, with a weather-board belfry capped by a branch spire. (The smallest church in use in England is Brenilham Church, Foxley, near Malmesbury, Wiltshire, which measures twelve feet square).

While seeking out the diminutive, take a look at Smugglers' Cottage, Northiam - by the A28 on the left as you drive south. It's a one-up, one-down building, claimed to be the smallest house in Sussex, yet it was once home to a family of five.

HEATHFIELD

GIBRALTAR TOWER

Access: In the (private) grounds of Heathfield Park, best seen from B2203. *Map reference:* TQ588214

'Calpes Defensori', or 'To the defender of Gibraltar', reads the inscription on the sadly neglected tower in Heathfield Park. Brigadier General George Augustus Elliott, who lived at the big house here, held the Rock against a siege by France and Spain between 1779 and 1783. He was later created Baron Heathfield. Three years after his death in 1792, Francis Newbury built this three-storey circular tower, 55 ft-high, to commemorate his exploits.

According to a contemporary report in *The Gentlemen's Magazine,* the tower's three apartments were 'to be fitted up in a Gothic style, and ornamented with views of Gibraltar and the operation of the Siege'. The letters of 'Calpes Defensori' were said to be made of metal from the guns of the Spanish floating batteries.

HEATHFIELD

NATURAL GAS PIPE - AN INDUSTRIAL RELIC

Access: In the trees near the bridge in Ghyll Road, north-west from Sandy Cross on the B2203
Map reference: TQ581206

This humble stand-pipe is the last remnant of Heathfield's natural gas industry, which produced some 15 million cubic feet a day in its heyday and provided the railway station with lighting until the 1930s. A commemorative medallion struck for the coronation of Edward VII and Queen Alexandra had the royal heads on one side and, on the other, 'Heathfield, Sussex, 1902. Natural gas first used for light and power.' The gas field had been discovered in 1895 while engineers were looking for water. Unfortunately the operation never proved commercially viable.

CADE STREET

JACK CADE MEMORIAL

Access: Along B2096 from A265 at Heathfield. The memorial is on your left.
Map reference: TQ607209

Jack Cade gave his name to the rebellion of 1450, leading an army of insurgents to London, seizing the Tower of London and beheading the Treasurer, Lord Saye. A weather-worn early 19th-century plaque recounts his fate, and it's echoed on a modern metal sign below:

Near this spot was slain the notorious rebel Jack Cade by Alexander Iden, Sheriff of Kent, A.D. 1450. His body was carried to London and his head fixed upon London Bridge. This is the success of all rebels, and this fortune chanceth ever to traitors.

40

CADE STREET

HARMER TERRACOTTA

> Access: In the graveyard of Cade Street Chapel, north-east of Old Heathfield.
> Take the B2096, south-east of the A265.
> *Map reference:* TQ614206

Nobody ever learned the secret of Jonathan Harmer's terracotta bas-reliefs, which have stood up to the weather remarkably well for close on two centuries. His father was a Heathfield stonemason, and Jonathan specialised in making these attractive ornaments for tombstones made by the family firm, which he took over in 1799. Their colours vary from cream to red, and there's a small range of designs, including cherubs, vases and baskets of fruit.

The terracottas can be seen in more than a dozen churchyards in the Heathfield area, and a small exhibition features them in Anne of Cleves House museum, Lewes.

BRIGHTLING

MAD JACK'S PYRAMID

> *Access:* In the churchyard at Brightling, 6 miles east of Heathfield.
> *Map reference:* TQ 684210

John "Mad Jack" Fuller (1757-1834) inherited the family mansion, Rose Hill, in Brightling on his twentieth birthday in 1777. He became M.P. for East Sussex and soon gained a reputation for being outspoken and an eccentric. He was also a patron of the arts and a public benefactor who provided Belle Tout lighthouse at East Dean (see page 29). However, he is best known for the many follies he erected around his estate in Brightling Park, after his retirement from politics, possibly to relieve unemployment in the area.

The follies include: The Rotunda Temple designed by Sir Robert Smirke in the grounds of Brightling Park; Brightling Needle, 65 ft. high, probably erected to celebrate the Battle of Waterloo in 1815; and the Observatory also designed by Smirke. However, the most unusual folly is the Pyramid, a 25ft-high mausoleum built in 1811 many years before his death, which stands in the churchyard, bizarre and rather ugly. A verse of Gray's *Elegy written in a County Churchyard,* is inscribed on one wall.

There is, sadly, no truth in the rumour that he was buried sitting on an iron chair in full evening dress, with a bottle of port and a roast chicken on the table in front of him, awaiting the Resurrection. He is buried beneath the pyramid.

Inside Brightling Church is the largest barrel organ in Britain. It was built in 1820 and is in full working order.

WOOD'S CORNER, NEAR DALLINGTON

THE SUGAR LOAF

> *Access:* Just off the B2096, 5 miles eeast of Heathfield.
> *Map reference:* TQ669195

The Sugar Loaf is said to have been designed to win a bet. While carousing at his home one night, the story goes, Jack Fuller wagered that he could see the spire of Dallington church from his top window. Since the sober light of day revealed that he couldn't, he swiftly had a new folly run up to fool his guest the next time he visited.

The odd building stands about forty feet high with a narrow entrance facing north-east and a single window due north. At its base the walls are eighteen inches thick, and its beaten-earth floor is about fourteen feet in diameter. In the late 19th century, the building was used as a two-storey cottage for a farmworker. The Sugar Loaf was saved from demolition by public subscription and restored in 1961. It takes its name from the similarity to the shape in which sugar was delivered to grocers.

MAYFIELD

VILLAGE SIGN

Access: In the High Street, just above the church.
Map reference: TQ586270

Those figures crouched beneath the name on Mayfield's colourful village sign are St. Dunstan and the Devil. Dunstan, a blacksmith by trade, built Mayfield's first wooden church in 960 A.D. He became Archbishop of Canterbury from 960-988, and he founded the Old Palace, close to the church. Legend tells that he had a forge in the village and that the Devil came to tempt him in the guise of a pretty girl. Fortunately Dunstan spotted a cloven hoof and seized his adversary's nose in a pair of red-hot tongs. The Devil promised never to enter a house with a horseshoe over its door.

The village sign, wich was second prize of £500 in a national newspaper competition in 1920, depicts a young woman and children in a flower-covered meadow, indicating that the original name of the village was Maid's Field, Maegthe (Saxon) and Maghefeld (1295).

The Victorian poet, Coventry Patmore, called Mayfield 'the sweetest village in England.'

HERSTMONCEUX

TELESCOPE DOMES

Access: Take the marsh road from Pevensey through Wartling. Immediately
before the entrance to Herstmonceux Castle (private) on your left,
there's a footpath giving an excellent view of the domes.
Map reference: TQ652104

The abandonment of Herstmonceux by the Royal Greenwich Observatory has given these
disused telescope domes something of an eery look. The RGO came to Sussex from
Greenwich in 1948 because the bright lights and polluted skies of London made
observation difficult. During the 1980s its main telescope was sited on the island of La
Palma in the Canary Islands and the work of the telescopes here became less vital. By the
end of the decade the decision was taken to move once again, to Cambridge.

*Make a slight detour to the village of Wartling and visit the small church. Inside is a very
unusual lectern in the shape of a heron, rather than the usual eagle. The birds have nested in
the parish for more than a century.*

HALLAND

BOW BELLS MILESTONE

Access: On the left-hand side of the A22, north-west of Halland.
Map reference: TQ495175

There's a string of so-called Bow Bells milestones along the A22 from Lingfield as far as Hailsham, a distance of 30 miles. There are more on the A26 between Uckfield and Lewes, and also between East Grinstead and Forest Row. These 'rebus' or puzzle milestones are, of course, a punning reference to the bells of Bow Church in the City of London, where most southbound roads from London were officially measured. From Uckfield and Horsebridge on the A22 there's an additional piece of ornamentation: a buckle above the number. This was the crest of the Pelham family which owned a great deal of the land through which the turnspike passed during the 18th century.

ASHDOWN FOREST

WHERE WINNIE-THE-POOH PLAYED

Access: Follow the bridleway from the Gill's Lap parking area on the B2026. You come to a pond on your right (Gill's Lap itself) and the land soon falls away. The memorial is on the left, behind trees.
Map reference: TQ468320

If you thought Winnie-the-Pooh, Tigger and company had their adventures in a completely imaginary place, you were wrong. This was the spot. 'By and by', wrote A.A. Milne, 'they came to an enchanted place on the very top of the Forest called Galleons Lap'. The words appear on memorial plaque to Milne and his illustrator, E.H. Shepard, 'who collaborated in the creation of Winnie-the-Pooh and so captured the magic of Ashdown Forest and gave it to the world'. The real name of the place is Gill's Lap.

Now how about playing Pooh-sticks where the famous game was invented? Travel to Hartfield, situated between East Grinstead and Tunbridge Wells. Locate Hartfield Garage, and about almost exactly opposite there is a road with restricted vehicular access. About half a mile down this road is a small wooden bridge over a stream, renovated in recent years by the county council, with the help of the publishers of Winnie-the-Pooh, Methuen. Go on: throw a twig over the side!

Complete your visit to Hartfield with a visit to 'Pooh Corner' at the south end of Hartfield High Street. The Tudor building, over 400 years old, contains a shop specialising in Winnie-the-Pooh. Open every day, but closed on Sunday and Monday morning.

ASHDOWN FOREST

NUTLEY POST MILL

Access: Take the Crowborough road north of Nutley. From the first car park on your left, a walk of a few hundred yards. The mill is occasionally open to the public during the season.

Map reference: TQ451291

This is the smallest open-trestle post mill in Sussex; one of only five surviving in the whole country. All the early mills were of the post variety, the whole building revolving round one huge post in order that the sweeps should face the wind. Later post mills had the space beneath enclosed within a roundhouse, which was used for storage, but at Nutley the supporting trestles are all on view.

The mill probably dates from around 1700 but moved from Crowborough to its present site during the 1830s. It was restored in the 1970s and won a European Architechtural Heritage Year award.

ASHDOWN FOREST

THE AIRMEN'S GRAVE

> *Access:* From the Hollies car park on the Crowborough road north of Nutley, take the left hand bridleway and walk downhill for about a mile.
> *Map reference:* TQ458274

Despite its popular name, this is actually a memorial rather than a grave. It was erected by the mother of Sgt. Pilot Victor Ronald Sutton, whose Wellington bomber crashed here in 1941, while returning from a raid on Cologne. The inscription reads: 'To the glorious memory of Sgt/PVR Sutton, aged 24 years, 142 Bom. Sqdn. R.A.F., also his five comrades who lost their lives through enemy action. 31.7.41. Mother.' A wreath is laid at the site every Remembrance Sunday.

There's a similar, if less elaborate, memorial five miles east of Heathfield by the road which runs from Wood's Corner to Bodle Street. A cross was erected by the mother of Flying Officer Peter Crofts, shot down here on September 28, 1940.

HOLTYE

ROMAN ROAD

Access: From a lay-by 300 yards east of the White Horse Inn on the south side of the A264, Signposted.
Map reference: TQ462387

The Romans constructed three main roads from London into Sussex, and at Holtye you can see part of the London-Lewes Way. This was principally an industrial route, linking the corn-growing South Downs area with the capital and providing outlets for the Wealden iron industry through the ports. A short stretch of the road has been excavated and is on view: iron slag was used for the metalling, and it was pounded and watered until it rusted into a solid mass.

ERIDGE

SAXONBURY TOWER

Access: On Saxonbury Hill in Eridge Park, eight miles north of Heathfield. The tower, situated on private land, is best seen from the minor road which runs under Saxonbury Hill from the A267, north of Mark Cross towards Eridge Green.
Map reference: TQ575330

This 19th-century folly now stands in a decayed state amid the wreckage of the 1987 'hurricane': huge beeches and pines lie across the paths of Saxonbury Wood. But it is, as luck has it, one of those romantic creations best seen from a distance. The tower, on land owned by the Marquis of Abergavenny and built to mark the highest point of the estate, is inscribed with the date 1828, and the letters *HA* appear over the door under a coronet.

Inside, the tower is very dilapidated, and the spiral stone staircase starts about eight feet from ground level.

The Nevill family, the most powerful in England in the later Middle Ages, has been connected with Sussex since the 15th century, when Sir Edward Nevill married Lady Elizabeth Beauchamp. She brought with her the Burgavenny title which was later changed to Abergavenny.

ERIDGE

ABERGAVENNY INSIGNIA

Access: Nevill Crest & Gun Public House on the A26.
Map reference: TQ558357

All around the Eridge area you can see the heraldic device of the Marquess of Abergavenny, whose home is at Eridge Park – a bull with Tudor rose and portcullis and a large 'A' tiled with tassels. The Punning family motto is *Ne Vile Velis: 'Wish No Evil'*.

Look out for the device at Rodmell, near Lewes. The family is recorded as owning the village in 1439, and the freehold of the manor was sold by the then Lord Abergavenny as recently as 1919. St. Peter's Place, Lewes, was developed by Lord Nevill in 1868, and the family has left its mark there, too.

BELLS YEW GREEN

BAYHAM ABBEY RUINS

Access: Off the B2169 about two miles east of Bells Yew Green.
Map reference: TQ649365

Bayham is one of those abbey ruins which owe their survival to their picturesque effect in the grounds of a rich man's house. This was the building now known as the Dower House, originally a mid-18th century Gothic villa, but enlarged by the first Marquess Camden. The architect and garden designer Humphrey Repton advised some landscaping of the site, but the remains are substantial enough to make it clear how the monks lived here from 1199 until its suppression in the 16th century.

NEWHAVEN

THOMAS TIPPER'S TOMBSTONE

Access: In St. Michael's churchyard.
Map reference: TQ444012

George IV was partial to the ale brewed by Thomas Tipper, a Newhaven character of the 18th century. He has an unusual inscription on his gravestone:

Reader, with kind regard this Grave survey,
Nor heedless pass where TIPPER'S ashes lay;
Honest he was, ingenuous, blunt, and kind;
And dared to, what few dare do, speak his mind.
PHILOSOPHY and HISTORY well he knew,
Was versed in PHYSICK and in SURGERY too.
The best old STINGO he both brewed and sold;
Nor did one knavish act to get his Gold.
He played through Life a varied comic part,
And knew immortal HUDIBRAS by heart.
Reader, in real truth, such was the Man;
Be better, wiser, laugh more if you can.

He was a prime mover in having a draw-bridge built over the Ouse at Newhaven, and there's an engraving of it at the top of the stone.

PIDDINGHOE

BRICK KILN

Access: In a garden by the Lewes-Newhaven road.
Map reference: TQ433032

This is the only bottle-shaped, brick-built kiln to survive anywhere in Sussex. It last functioned in 1912, and the brickworks are now largely buried under the road which bypasses the village. The kiln was restored in 1980 after first being completely dismantled.

Piddinghoe church has one of the only three Norman round towers in Sussex (the others being at St Michael's, Lewes, and at Southease). In his poem 'Sussex', Kipling described the weathervane as a 'begilded dolphin'. His eyesight was notoriously bad: it's a salmon trout.

SEAFORD

MARTELLO TOWER

Access: Follow the coast road from the A259 for about a mile. Situated on the sea-front, close to Seaford Head.
Map reference: TV485985

A string of Martello towers was constructed along the south and east coasts of England against possible Napoleonic invasion, and the one at Seaford (No. 74), built in 1806, was the most westerly of them all. The tower has seen many uses over the years: a Customs station, a Coastguard look-out, Observer Corps post, roller-skating rink, in the dry moat, a private house – with an additional floor built on top of the tower, and an ice-cream and tea shop situated within the protective sea wall in front of the tower. In 1979, the tower became the new home of the Seaford Museum of Local History, covering 6,000 square feet of floor space and including many fascinating displays. Notice the gun platform on the roof.

BISHOPSTONE

SAXON SUNDIAL

Access: Bishopstone Church, signposted off A259 west of Seaford.
Map reference: TQ472010

Who Eadric was we don't know, but his name is inscribed on a rare Saxon sundial over the entrance porch of St. Andrew's Church, Bishopstone. The lines on the dial mark the four 'tides' of the day and their division into three parts. There would once have been a gnomon protruding from the centre hole, casting a shadow when the sun was out, but very few of these remain today.

Bishopstone served as a retreat for the Bishops of Chichester, who stayed in the village until the 17th century.

TIDE MILLS

OLD WORKINGS

Access: Via a narrow roadway off the A259 Seaford to Newhaven road.
Map reference: TQ459002

A messy site, but fascinating for anyone interested in industrial archaeology. A tide mill was built here in 1762 by William Catt and operated until 1890. Harnessing the power of the incoming tides and storing water for when the sea retreated, it was able to operate for all of sixteen hours a day. A small settlement grew up here and, despite the primitive conditions, it was inhabited until the second world war. During the war, the area was used for artillery practice. You can see an abandoned railway halt, the footings of former cottages and three wheel tunnels in the dam, with fragments of the sluice gates.

PEACEHAVEN

MERIDIAN MONUMENT

> *Access:* At the bottom of Horsham Avenue, off the A259 – Newhaven to Brighton coast road.
> *Map reference:* TQ922203

The Greenwich Meridian passes through Sussex and Peacehaven. Its exact position was established by Commander Davenport R.N., who erected the first monument – a wooden structure with a large star and four distance signposts. A new one, overlooking the sea, was unveiled in 1936 by Charles Neville, the colourful developer of Peacehaven. The 20ft-high memorial is of white stone on a base of York stone, topped by a copper sphere with a bronze rod pointing to the north star. There are two plaques, one inscribed with the distances from various far-flung parts of the empire, and the other to the memory of King George V.

Charles Neville bought the land here during the first world war, laid out a grid of streets and building plots and advertised a new 'garden city by the sea'. It attracted pioneering types prepared to accept the most basic standards of sanitation, water provision and power supply, but its haphazard bungaloid growth has given the place a bad name among planners

Other Meridian markers include two in Lewes: in Western Road and on the Landport Estate.

LEWES

ANCHORESS'S CELL

> *Access:*   In St Anne's church at the very top of High Street.
> *Map reference:* TQ409100

An anchoress once lived in a cell here. St Richard of Chichester left money in his will of 1253 to 'include Beate Marie de Westoute apud Lewenses' – the woman recluse of St Mary's, Westoute at Lewes. Peering through the bars you get some idea of what it must have been like to be walled up for the good of mankind. There's a hatch in the south chapel through which she would have received her food.

Close to the lychgate in the churchyard is a curious tombstone which nobody has ever been able to explain. It's to 'little Benjamin the Ruler', who died in 1747 at the age of 89. His name isn't in the church register.

LEWES

18th-CENTURY MILESTONE

Access: Set in the wall of the half-timbered second-hand bookshop near the
traffic lights half way up High Street.
*Map reference:*TQ411100

A late 18th-century milestone in a 15th-century building. It reads:

50 MILES

FROM THE STANDARD

IN CORNHILL.

49 TO WESTMINSTER BRIDGE

8 MILES TO BRIGHTHELMSTONE

Brighthelmstone was the former name for Brighton.

LEWES

TOAD IN THE HOLE

Access: In the Lewes Arms, Mount Place, off Fisher Street.
Map reference: TQ411102

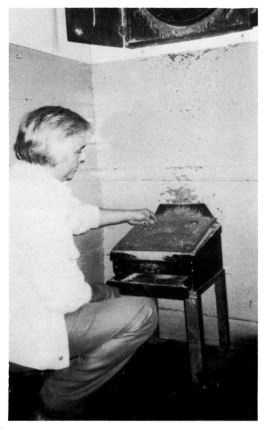

Traditional pub games are now to be found almost exclusively in museums, but this ancient Toad in the Hole at the Lewes Arms is still regularly in use. The aim is to throw heavy discs into a hole in the centre of the slanted lead top, which has become heavily dented over the years. The scoring? Two points if you sink the disc, one if it comes to rest on the top.

A more elaborate form of the game can be seen in Horsham museum in West Sussex; this is taller, has a number of holes and boasts a model toad with invitingly open mouth.

Another Lewes pub, the Snowdrop Inn (in South Street, near the southern entrance of the Cuilfail Tunnel), takes its name from a tragedy rather than from the flower. On Christmas Eve 1836 eight people were killed in Britain's worst avalanche disaster. The pub sign shows men with spades trying to dig the victims out.

LEWES

CZAR ALEXANDER'S OBELISK

Access: In the churchyard of St John Sub Castro.
Map reference: TQ415105

During the Crimean War many captured Finns were held at the old Naval prison in Lewes, and twenty eight of them died here. In 1877 Czar Alexander II, who was Grand Duke of Finland, raised this obelisk to their memory.

While in Lewes the prisoners made interlooking wooden puzzles which they sold to the locals, and some of these can be seen in the Anne of Cleves House Museum.

LEWES

A CARPENTER'S GRAVESTONE

Access: In the churchyard of St John sub Castro
Map reference: TQ415105

No marks for guessing the trade of Mark Sharp, who died in 1747. His carpenters' tools are carved, with great detail, on the footstone of his grave outside St John sub Castro. A case of one craftsman honouring another.

Note, set into the outside wall of the south aisle, the chancel arch of the church which preceded the existing one. It commemorates, in medieval Lombardic lettering, a Danish warrior who became an anchorite here.

LEWES

THE MARTYRS' MEMORIAL

Access: On the Downs above the town. Either take the ramp through the Cuilfail estate from Cliffe or, for a prettier walk, climb Chapel Hill and follow the footpath signs. This latter route takes you right up to the memorial but the wrong side of a wire fence.
Map reference: TQ424104

The Lewes bonfire celebrations on November 5 are the most violent and colourful in the country, and there's always a no-Popery element to the proceedings. This is an echo through the centuries of the Protestant fervour which saw seventeen people burned to death in Lewes during the sixteenth century. Their memorial stands high above the town:

IN LOVING MEMORY
OF THE UNDERNAMED
SEVENTEEN PROTESTANT
MARTYRS,
WHO, FOR THEIR FAITHFUL
TESTIMONY TO
GOD'S TRUTH,
WERE, DURING THE REIGN OF
QUEEN MARY,
BURNED TO DEATH
IN FRONT OF THE THEN STAR
INN - NOW THE TOWN HALL -
LEWES,
THIS OBELISK,
PROVIDED BY PUBLIC
SUBSCRIPTIONS,
WAS ERECTED A.D. 1901.

ASHCOMBE

TOLL HOUSE

Access: By the A27 just west of Lewes on the south side.
Map reference: TQ389093

It looks rather like an ice house, but this is one of a pair of tollhouses which once sat on either side of the Lewes-Brighton road. The other was demolished for road widening. The building, dating from about 1810, was too small ever to have been lived in.

ALCISTON

TITHE BARN

Access: The village is signposted off the A27. The barn is close to the church.
Map reference: TQ505055

The land around Alciston was once owned by Battle Abbey, which no doubts explains the size of the medieval tithe barn. With a length of 170ft., it's one of the largest in Sussex, and it's still in use – though not, of course, for gathering a tenth of every neighbour's produce.

This is a beautiful, sequestered spot. The barn forms a group with an ancient (and dilapidated) stone dovecote and the parish church of St. Mary.

Patcham, on the northern outskirts of Brighton, boasts an even larger tithe barn but, save for the wooden beams inside, little more than the footings have survived modernisation. At Wilmington Priory the base of the tithe barn remains, to form the car park.

GLYNDE

A PALLADIAN CHURCH

Access: Take the A27 Lewes to Polegate Road, turn off to Glynde and the church stands on the right.
Map reference: TQ456093

This distinctive church was built in 1763 by the man who lived next door to it in Glynde Place – Richard Trevor, Bishop of Durham. He chose the site of an earlier, medieval church, but had his built in a Palladian style unusual for a small parish church. Among the surprises inside are the hessian wall coverings.

In the churchyard is the tomb of John Ellman (1753-1832), which tells us that 'by him the breed of Southdown sheep was first improved and thro his exertions spread over the whole kingdom'.

LAUGHTON

LAUGHTON PLACE

> *Access:* On the B2124 east from Ringmer take the first right turn after passing
> Broyle Place on your left. Turn right again along a farm track, and the
> tower is about a mile further on.
> *Map reference:* TQ485114

The story goes that young Sir John Pelham helped capture King of France at Poitiers in
1356, and that after the spoils were divided someone had the idea of giving the lad a
buckle. This is probably a myth, but a buckle is certainly the emblem of the Pelham
family. You'll see one on this rather remote tower which, apart from the moat, is all that
remains of the family's original home, last rebuilt here in 1534.

FIRLE

GAMEKEEPER'S TOWER

Access: Take the small road marked Firle Place from the A27 near Middle Farm. A footpath runs fairly close to the tower.

Map reference: TQ481072

This was built by Lord Gage in 1819 as accommodation for the gamekeeper on the Firle Estate: pheasant were reared in this area, for shooting in the autumn. It had inside a circular kitchen, a circular drawing room and, to quote its present occupant, 'three bedrooms like slices of Dutch cheese'.

It also acted as a signalling tower. When the 4th Viscount Gage was returning home by train his manservant would flutter a white handkerchief from the window of their carriage. A flag would then be flown from the tower, and carriage would immediately set off from Firle Place to meet the party at Glynde station. The gamekeeper could also sign with flags to his men on the estate and communicate by telegraph with the keeper at Plashett Park, Ringmer, five miles away.

BERWICK

BLOOMSBURY WALLPAINTINGS

Access: In the church
Map reference: TQ519049

This is Bloomsbury territory. Virginia Woolf lived at Rodmell, near Lewes, and her sister, Vanessa Bell, at Charleston Farmhouse under Firle Beacon. After Berwick church had its windows blown out by a German bomb in the last war, Bishop Bell of Chichester suggested to the Rector that Vanessa, her son Quentin and her lover, Duncan Grant, should be asked to paint the walls of the church. The Nativity painting in the nave (as shown) painted by Vanessa and Quentin, is a local scene, incorporating a Sussex trug, a Southdown lamb , a Pyecombe crook, a Sussex barn and Mount Caburn, near Lewes. The faces are local, too; the models for the painting included two shepherds, the artists' gardener and the son of their housekeeper.

RODMELL

VIRGINIA WOOLF MEMORIAL

Access: In the garden of Monks House (National Trust), signposted off the
Lewes-Newhaven road.
Map reference: TQ422053

After the novelist Virginia Woolf took her life in 1941, drowning in the River Ouse, her
ashes were scattered under an elm just beyond the garden of Monks House. The plaque
which her husband, Leonard, raised to her memory is now inside the garden. It has a
quotation from her novel 'The Waves':

> *"Death is the enemy. Against you*
> *I will fling myself unvanquished*
> *and unyielding – O Death!"*
> *The waves broke on the shore.*

Monks House is opened by the National Trust, twice a week during the summer months
only.

RINGMER

TIMOTHY TORTOISE

Access: Village sign on the A26 from Lewes
Map reference: TQ445124

Timothy tortoise is the star of the Ringmer village sign. The famous naturalist Gilbert White made something of a study of the creature on his visits to its owner, his aunt Rebecca Snooke. After her death he adopted Timothy, whose shell is now preserved at the British Museum.

Playing second fiddle to the tortoise are two other famous men, both of whom married local women – William Penn, the Quaker and founder of Pennsylvania; and John Harvard, founder of the American university.

Tortoise lovers are directed towards the Frankland memorial in STANMER Park. (See Page 83).

KINGSTON

DEWPONDS

> *Access:* Take the Kingston turn from the Lewes-Newhaven road and turn left up Kingstonridge at the far end of the village before the road descends in a cut to the A27. A footpath climbs steeply, with the first dewpond on your left soon after reaching the summit. For the second one, a conservation project, turn left along the South Downs Way.
> *Map reference:* TQ379079; TQ383078

Dewponds are scattered all along the Downs, traditionally made of puddled clay and holding rain water which otherwise would sink rapidly through the porous chalk. Kipling wrote of 'the dewpond on the height/Unfed, that never fails', but perhaps he had yet to experience a serious drought. Certainly the ponds need to be maintained: this one was wet enough when the photograph was taken, but vegetation was threatening to smother it.

OFFHAM

CHALKPIT RAILWAY

Access: Alongside the car park of the Chalk Pit public house on the A275 from Lewes.

Map reference: TQ400116

This is sometimes called the first railway in south-east England, which suggests the most terrifying of white-knuckle rides. The wagons which dropped 400 feet down a 1-in-2 incline were, however, carrying chalk. You can still see the four lime kilns from the days when this was a working chalkpit. The wagons disappeared under the road and emerged to end at a wharf on a cut from the River Ouse. The railway was built in 1809 and was in use until 1870.

STREAT

THE 'V' PLANTATION

> *Access:*   Best seen from the south end of Streat Lane on the B2116 between
> Plumpton and Westmeston.
> *Map reference:* TQ348130

People found all sorts of ways to celebrate Queen Victoria's diamond Jubilee in 1897, but
none can have been more imaginative than this – a plantation of trees in the shape of a 'V'.

NEWICK

VILLAGE PUMP

Access: On the village green, just off the A272
Map reference: TQ419213

A village pump in working order is something of a rarity. This one was erected by local residents in 1897 – to celebrate Queen Victoria's jubilee. A notice on its front forbids its use for the filling of steam engines.

BRIGHTON

THE ROYAL PAVILION

Access: Old Steine, a short way up the A23 London Road from the sea-front.
Map reference: TQ313042

'A collection of stone pumpkins and pepper boxes' is how the writer William Hazlitt described this most notable example of over-the-top seaside architecture. There is, in fact, a much more sedate building hidden inside it. The colourful Prince Regent (later George IV) employed the architect John Nash to rebuild it in the flamboyant pseudo Oriental style which makes the Royal Pavilion, completed in 1821, an exotic spectacle both outside and in.

An excerpt from an 1820 satire *The Joss and his Folly* by William Hone mirrors public opinion:

The queerest of all the queer sights
I've set sight on;-
Is, the *what d'ye-call-'t thing,* here,
THE FOLLY at Brighton
The outside - huge teapots,
all drill'd round with holes,
Relieved by extinguishers,
sticking on poles:
The inside - all tea - things,
and dragons, and bells,
The show rooms - all show,
the sleeping rooms - cells.

But the *grand* Curiosity
's not to be seen -
The owner himself -
an old fat MANDARIN;
A patron of painters
who copy designs
That grocers and tea-dealers
hang up for signs:
hence teaboard -taste artists
gain rewards and distinction.
Hence his title of 'Teapot'
Shall last to extinction.

BRIGHTON

PHOEBE HESSEL'S GRAVE

Access: In the churchyard of St Nicholas at the top of Church Street.
Map reference: TQ307045

It's fitting that the simple inscription *P. Hessel* conceals the gender of this grave's inhabitant, since the remarkable Phoebe is renowned for a spectacularly impressive feat of disguise. Determined not to be separated from. the man she loved, she followed him into the Army. No doubt she embellished the story over the years (she lived to 108), but she claimed to have passed for a man during 17 years of service; to have fought in the 5th Regiment of Foot; and to have been wounded at Fontenoy. Happily, she did marry her man.

Another redoubtable Brighton character is buried nearby: Martha Gunn, most famous of the original female bathing attendants, the 'dippers'. She began her beach duties in 1750 and continued performing them until shortly before her death in 1815 at the age of 89.

BRIGHTON

VOLK'S ELECTRIC RAILWAY

> *Access:* Madeira Drive.
> *Map reference:* TQ318038

Magnus Volk (1851-1937) invented all kinds of electrical and mechanical gadgets, including the installation of electric light in the Royal Pavilion in 1883. The same year, he received permission from the Brighton Corporation to open an electric railway, the first in Britain, on the sea-front for a trial period of six months. The 2 ft. gauge track ran from near the Aquarium to the Old Chain Pier. The railway proved a success and it was extended to Black Rock in 1901. Here it is, still carrying passengers east from the Palace Pier as it did in 1883. Most of the cars date from 1897-1901.

BRIGHTON

PEPPER POT

Access: Tower Road, close to Queen's Park.
Map reference: TQ324043

The Pepper Pot, as it's long been known, once stood in the grounds of a villa designed for Thomas Attree by the architect of the House of Commons, Sir Charles Barry. It was used as an observation tower during the second world war, but its original purpose (other than to look striking) isn't known. The villa itself was completed in 1830 and demolished in the 1970s.

Note, a little to the east, a small kiosk at the entrance to the Carn Court block of flats. This was Attree's garden temple.

BRIGHTON

ROYAL SPA

> *Access:* In the South-west corner of Queen's Park.
> *Map reference:* TQ321044

Brighton isn't known as a spa town, but Dr. F.A. Struve opened an artificial one here in 1825 on the lines of others he had successfully developed in Berlin, Leipzig and his home town of Dresden. He concocted mineral waters which were chemically identical to those of European spas. A royal warrant was granted in 1835, and the amenity was thereafter known as the Royal Spa. The pump room has gone, but the Ionic portico and the north wall have been restored.

STANMER

FRANKLAND MONUMENT

> *Access:* Among the trees south west of the spot where the road divides in Stanmer Park.
> *Map reference:* TQ338092

Three tortoises (now headless) support this monument, which is made of artificial Coade stone. The inscription reads:

> *To the Memory of*
> *Frederick Frankland esq., M.P.*
> *died March th 8th, 1768 aged 73;*
> *This Monument is erected by his*
> *ever affectionate and most truly*
> *grateful son and daughter*
> *Thomas Lord Pelham and Ann*
> *his wife June 1775.*

The Pelhams were the first Earl and Countess of Chichester, and the obelisk commemorates her father.

Why the tortoises? Similar designs can be found elsewhere in the country, which suggests that the Pelhams made a choice from a pattern-book.

PATCHAM

A SMUGGLER'S TOMBSTONE

Access: In the churchyard to the north of the church.
Map reference: TQ303092

Here's evidence that smuggling was once regarded as acceptable behaviour by the public at large. The now-faded verse reads, in part;

All ye who do this stone draw near,
Oh! Pray let fall the pitying tear,
From the sad instance may we all
Prepare to meet Jehovah's call.

Poor Daniel Skayles was 'unfortunately shot' by a mounted customs officer when his gang was caught with a load of contraband.

Take a look, in this connection, at Burnt Cottage in East Dean Road, Eastbourne. A plaque shows that it was 'rebuilt by public subscription' - after Revenue officers set fire to the original building because its cellars were used for storing smuggled goods. No doubt here about what the locals thought of the law.

PATCHAM

THE CHATTRI

Access: Through a farmyard north of Vale Avenue, following signs to Standean Farm. After about 200 yards, a (well marked) footpath veers off to the left and climbs the Downs for more than a mile. A key giving access to the Chattri grounds is obtainable at Patcham Lodge, immediately opposite the Black Lion public house on London Road.
Map reference: TQ304111

The Royal Pavilion was used as a hospital during the first world war, and the bodies of the Indian soldiers who died there were cremated at a 'ghat' 500ft. above sea level on the Downs. In 1921 the Chattri was erected on the site as their memorial. The inscription reads:

To the memory of all the Indian Soldiers who gave their lives in the services of their King Emperor in the Great War this monument erected on the site of the funeral pyre where the Hindus and Sikhs who died in hospital at Brighton passed through the fire is in grateful admiration and brotherly affection dedicated.

Around the Chattri is a two-acre garden.

HOVE

AN ENGINEER'S FOLLY

Access: In the grounds of the British Engineerium, off Nevill Road.
Map reference: TQ286066

Some large and unusual flints came from the wells and adits dug out when a pumping station was built in Hove in the 1860s. The chief water engineer obviously thought they shouldn't go to waste, for he fashioned his own folly from them – a construction of arches with a small scalloped cavern, now romantically clad with ivy.

The British Engineerium, founded in 1975, houses hundreds of full size and model steam engines. The exhibition is open all the year round from 10 a.m. to 5 p.m. and in steam on Sundays and Bank Holidays.

HANGLETON

DOVECOTE

Access: Hangleton Valley Drive, Hove.
Map reference: TQ265069

This 17th-century dovecote stands in the grounds of the oldest domestic secular building in Brighton and Hove – Hangleton Manor, which was built in 1540. (The Manor is now a public house). The walls are several feet thick and there would once have been literally hundreds of nesting boxes inside, reached by a 'potence' or swinging ladder.

Other surviving dovecotes include those at Charleston Manor, near West Dean; in Motcombe Gardens, East-bourne; and (a scheduled ancient monument) at Patcham.

WEST BLATCHINGTON

SMOCK MILL

> *Access:* Follow the A2038 south-west from the Devil's Dyke roundabout north
> of Hove. The windmill lies in Holmes Avenue, just south of the road,
> and is signposted. It has a museum inside and is open on Sundays and
> Bank Holidays in the season.
> *Map reference:* TQ278068

This hexagonal smock mill appears to be built on top of a barn. In fact, its square tower goes down to ground level, with the barns built round it. An earlier mill dates back to 1724, but the present structure was built around 1820 and belonged to the Marquess of Abergavenny as part of West Blatchington Farm. The mill was painted by Constable in 1825 and for many years it was a landmark on Admiralty charts. The photograph shows it dressed for the 1991 village celebrations.

A smock mill is a wooden-framed, many-sided mill, with a movable cap. Most are octagonal, so that West Blatchington is a rarity. A fantail, a small secondary windmill installed at the rear of the cap, is geared to turn the cap to face the wind.

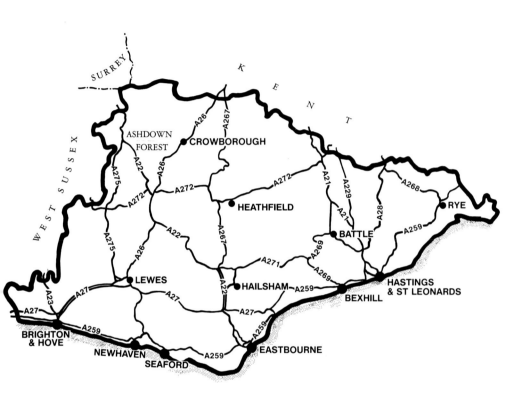

INDEX